The Girl Who was Saved by the Hands of God

by

Letrice Gandy

DORRANCE PUBLISHING CO
EST. 1920
PITTSBURGH, PENNSYLVANIA 15238

Dorrance Publishing Co
585 Alpha Drive
Pittsburgh, PA 15238
Visit our website at www.dorrancebookstore.com

ISBN: 979-8-88812-212-9
eISBN: 979-8-88812-712-4

My name is Letrice Nikole Gandy, and this is my autobiography of my life. I am sorry if it is a little hard to read, but it was even harder to live. I wish I could tell you my life was great, but that's just not the fact. Before I tell you everything, there is something you need to hear. No matter how bad your life is, no matter what has happened, no matter how bad things seem, you are never alone. It is only by the hands of God I lived to tell this. Many times I had no one but me and God. He pulled me up and carried me through some really hard times. He helped me before I even asked him to come into my life. He saw that I lived for some reason. God is real. He is amazing in every way. He loves you unconditionally no matter what. How cool is that? That our God can just be there and his presence can carry you there. I mean he never once lifted me; I was so weak at times and felt I would never make it, but God pulled me through. I know he was there. Sometimes you do not even need to ask the answers to your prayers, for me, even the unspoken ones.

Sometimes God will speak differently without words; he sends signs. And if you don't watch closely you will miss them. It's weird how God sometimes just shows up and provides. You never really know when or how, you just know he is there.

I will tell you I found forgiveness after a very long, long time. But I just can't forget. Someday this stuff just runs through my mind like a record. The pain, the mental anxiety I feel some days, I just want to shut down, forget about the world, lay in bed and die But I can't. I have to keep going. It's so important. You try, but sometimes it's not good enough. You gotta try harder. Life can knock you on your butt, but you get up. Try again. This is so hard to talk about, but I have to get it out.

I got cheated out of school and I never got my high diploma. But I promise you now I will make something out of myself. I will go back to school and college too. See, I have dreams. And no one can take them away. I will make it.

He knows when to be there. Of course he always is, but I mean he knows when you need that shield of protection.

I did not ask God into my life until I was sixteen. But in everything I believe he was still there. All the times I try to kill myself… if not, I would have been dead. And one more thing before you read this: I believe God has a special place for people with mental issues due to things that are not their fault. Or he holds them in a different accountability. I do not know that for sure, but that is how I feel. Just remember to keep the faith and remember God is always there. Praise him in all things you do. Let God be the first thing you think of when you wake up and the last thing you think of when you go to bed.

I wrote this not only to get closer in my life but to support others. May God help you to open your mind as you read this and bless your soul if you or anyone you know ever lived through this. So here we go!

I have lived a very hard life, but I choose to live. I could have given up anytime and let the devil win, but then where would I be today? Nowhere, maybe even dead. I chose it to fight to survive. I was playing a card game of spades and always got the duds. Never any high cards to play. But that's okay because I was going to make it in the end. Scared, lonely, yes, but I had God. Do not feel alone. Be strong and tell yourself you will succeed. Everyone can try to take your power but only if you allow them to. The mind is a great tool; use it to your benefit and use it wisely. You are not alone.

My childhood was very bad. I never asked to be born, but I paid for it every day of my life. I woke up every morning. I was not dealt the hand I was proud of. I dealt with emotional abuse and physical abuse. The abuse was really bad. I just could not tell the things I went through from my mother, her boyfriends and my grandparents. Some days I just wanted to run away. Sometimes I run away from myself. I got beat. Locked up in places where it was dark. Thrown around like a doll. Yes, we were kids, we did things wrong, but it never ever needed to be done like this. But we learned new things every day. One: we had to protect ourselves. Two: others had it better, and three: we were never alone. God was always there. I can't count the number of nights I prayed to God to take me home please. Why was he not answering? Then I came to terms with the fact that I was still alive. There was a reason for me to be here. Why? I don't know. I ask the same question every night.

My mother could do a lot to me, but she can't take God away. I never knew how important God was to me. Then I saw he was the only thing keeping me alive. Many days I went without food. But on those days, I believe I was fasting for the Lord. I would be hit if I said I was hungry. I often stole to get food. I felt really bad. And I was afraid the food would make me sick. I was way underweight. Way underweight. I just wished so badly for a normal life. Then sexual abuse from my mother's brother.

My mother was pregnant at fifteen with my sister and had me at sixteen. That's right, eleven months after, here I was. A mistake. I always was and always will be. My mother always used to say "I brought you into this world and I can take you out." But I learned that's not true. She may have given birth to me but she did not bring me here; God did. That made me mad. Every time she said that, it was a treat. I better be scared.

She married my dad at sixteen. I loved my dad a lot. He was very cool. I looked up to him. He tried to protect us as much as possible when Mom went crazy. I never felt like I belonged in the family. Maybe I really did not. Maybe I was switched at birth. My mom made sure of that, but my dad would always tell me he loved me and I was his boo boo. He never said things like that to my sister. I remember doing things with my dad. We had times together that I hold dear to my heart. He took me places and taught me things that no one else did. He always told me I was worth something. He was nothing like my mom. He treated me with respect and taught me values. He was hard, firm, strict but he loved me. He always let me try things on my own, but was there if I needed help. He never put me down. Always tell me you want something, you work for it. He fought all the time with my mom because my mom called me disabled and said I could not do things. My dad looked at me and said, "Can't never did anything." He looked at me and said, "Did you even try?"

I said, "Mom said I can't."

He said, "Prove her wrong."

So I did. My dad was proud. He took me in his arms and said, "I knew you could do anything. Please never give up on yourself."

From that day forward I knew my dad had the ability to be wise. I looked up and learned as much as I could. He held me close and kissed me for things done right and his hands were hard as steel when I did wrong. He always told me what I did wrong and tried to help me do right. My lessons were deep and did not come cheap but I learned. Like the time I took something that was not mine, my dad sat me down and told me what I did wrong and took the belt and whipped it across my butt ten times. Then he took me by the hand and made me return the item. He talked to me the whole way home telling me life lessons I needed to know. He said, "Do not fear anything. God is with you. Just ask him if I am not around."

I said, "God talks to you?"

He said, "Of course, always. You pray then listen. He hears your every need. And never leaves us."

I said, "Even when we do wrong?"

Dad said, "Nope. He wants us to ask for forgiveness."

I said, "How do I do that?"

My dad said, "Let me show you." He prayed with me. After we prayed my dad took me in his arms and said, "I love you boo boo, and I am sorry I whipped you."

I said, "It's okay, Daddy, I own what I did."

My dad hugged me and said, "You did not need the whipping. You taught me something."

I said, "I guess we are both still learning."

My dad said, "We sure are, baby girl. I did not hurt you badly?"

I said, "Daddy, stop worrying. I am okay."

He said, "I just feel bad."

I said, "I will live. I love you, Daddy."

He said, "I love you, baby boo."

From then on I felt different about my dad. We prayed often together. He taught me how to stay in the presence of the Lord and do right. I love him for that. He was my rock. He made me feel happy all the time. I was at peace with him and the Lord. Nothing could hurt me there.

Mom was crazy herself. I shut down a lot and stayed out of the way. I was afraid not to. I found a hiding spot where no one could get to me. I would stay there and sing and pray to myself. I even stole food and would eat there but they found out. So they trapped me there for three hours. I stopped going in there to live. Sometimes my sister, sometimes my few friends and a very nice person who lived by our creek. My sister called him Backwater Bob. He was a homeless man. But very kind. He never hurt me. We were friends. But my sister told my mom, and she followed me one day and treated him. He never talked to me again and my mom locked me in the garage for two days for that. She did that often as a punishment, but I did not mind that; it was my quiet time with the Lord. She called it my isolation room. I did get hungry and thirsty and had to sleep on the ground. But that was better than being beat. Not being seen or heard was a good chance of getting less abuse. Because if you got in the way you really got hurt. Sometimes you could not walk, other times you had whip marks everywhere.

I remember being beaten so badly with a paint stick wrapped in duct tape that we could not even take gym class the next day because we had marks up and down our legs and on our butts. I skipped school that day. I went to the baseball field with a boyfriend. I showed him my body. He said, "Let's run away. I said no. He felt so bad. He said, "I can hide you in my tree house." I said no and told him I had to go.

At the age of six months old, I almost died. Someone put bad milk in my bottle. I bet it was my mom. I hated her. She was the only one who wanted me dead. My sister, only eleven months older, stood at my bed holding my hand as I ran a very high temp. No one took me to get help. She would not leave my side. At least she cared.

We moved around for a short while my mom and dad could not find work. My dad did odd jobs. But he was very young. Never finished high school. So we went back to my grandparents' house and my parents split. I was so mad at my dad for leaving. Why could he have not taken me? What was wrong with me? He knew what my mom's family was like and he left me there. Thanks a lot, Dad. I owe you for that one. I know he had no job, but he was about ready to leave his child to be beat on, emotionally abused and sexually abused. So yes, I was very angry at him. Look at how he did me. He threw me away like trash. Did not care a thing about what was going to happen to me. Why should I even try anymore? The one thing I loved left me. He did not even turn around to say goodbye, say I love you or try to explain anything. He just took my heart and left. Fine by me, Daddy, who needs you, I thought.

That's when the abuse started. My grandparents would beat us with newspaper, belts, and wooden paint sticks wrapped in duct tape. They would leave marks all over us. They would dare us to tell anyone. I hated God so much. I hated my life. I had no will to live. I was young and scared. But most of all I didn't understand why people hated me. I felt like nobody wanted me. I didn't live like that. I needed help. I called my dad; he said he could not take me because he had no money and no job. SO YOU MAKE SOMETHING LIKE A KID BUT YOU CANNOT TAKE

WHEN IT IS BEING BEATEN? So I ran away. That was my first try. I was young, waiting for someone to help me. The police brought me back to my mom. She was mad. My mom hit me so hard I fell to the ground. Pain hit me like a ton of bricks. She grabbed me, pulled me upstairs to the bathroom, ripped my clothes off, turned the water on really hot and pushed me in. I screamed, "Mommy, hot!" It was so hot my skin was starting to turn blood red.

At the same time she was hitting me with a belt, a leather one. She was screaming, "You did this! Count out your licks!"

I tried but the pain was so bad.

She said, "We are not stopping until you count to fifty." I was not going to make it. She screamed, starting over. I counted again, not being able to get to 10, and I just fell. My mom said, "I knew it was over." She shut the water off and threw my washcloth and told me to dry off. Afterwards she went out to the garage to play pool with her lover.

My grandma came with towels and dried me off. She saw the marks and burns from the water. She said I was dumb and to never try that again. She got my clothes on me and got me to bed. Gave me two of mom's pain pills and I was asleep fast. She sat there asking God why. I asked to God in my own way. That night I prayed he would take me home. I don't know if God ever asked her.

I woke up the next morning still in pain. A lot of pain. It took me about four weeks to heal. I tried everything to feel better, but it would not work. When mom would go to work, I would take a few of her pills to help with the pain. My mom did not talk to me for days.

Mom finally did in a little while because she had enough money to move us next door. Why next door? Thank you, Mom. In a different house of course. But my grandparents had a key. They came in all while my mom was at work and beat us. She still worked at jobs so they had to take care of us. They really took care of us. We had a little more freedom. But all the doors with food were locked so we still had to eat sneak food. I never got any time alone. This bothered me. I just wanted so badly to be by myself. Sometimes I wished something would happen to my mom and she would not come home.

I found a dog and brought it home and wanted to keep it. Mom's boyfriend shot it. I cried for days. Mom gave me a bunny. I named him Thumper. He had a cage and food and everything. I took my allowance and bought him a leash. I took him outside. I had him for a long time. He died while I was at school one day. I came home and held him in my arms and cried. Mom said to her boyfriend, "We gotta get him away from her.". Mom tried to get him and I pulled away. My mom's boyfriend slapped me in the face and I dropped the bunny. My mom yelled at him and picked up the bunny and walked away. Later that day she tried to tell me things die, nothing lives forever.

On top of all this, my mother had boyfriends that would beat her when they drank. I remember being just six years old running across the street to the gas station to call 911 so they did not beat her to death. Sometimes I would act like I was asleep and just let them hit her, not often but I got tired of it.. That was no way to live. It was hell.

I also remember one night when my mom's boyfriend got drunk and put a knife all the way through his hand. He woke me up out of bed and said, "See, I told you I would do it."

I lived with this stuff all the time. I would hide in my closet when Mom and her boyfriends got drunk so I would not get hit. It was dark there. Sometimes it worked. Other times we would get the worst beating of our lives. Sometimes we would not even able to sit or walk for days.

I grew up mad at everyone. I used to stay out as late as I could so I never was home. I skipped school so my friends didn't see my marks on my body. I never took gym. I cut kills. I would cut on myself to relieve emotional pain, and I would run away from home. But the cops always found me. I remember I ran away for two days one time. When the cops brought me home, my mom beat me for two hours straight then made me sit in a hard chair all day. Did she not understand why I did not want to be there? That was the second time. I mean she beat me until I bled and kept going. I was hurting so bad. I cried for days. She took all my rights away. But the worst part was I was not allowed to see my dad for two months. I tried to fight her on that one but lost. Why take that away? I wanted my daddy so bad. When I saw him I was in heaven. I did all kinds of things with him. But I always had to go back home. I would act out when it was time to take me home. Dad just made me go away.

Then the worst was when in six years things really

changed for the worst. I could handle the beatings, but when my mother's brother started touching me it did something to me. At first it was foul play. You know, rubbing me, whipping my butt, playing with my jugs. Then he went too far. My mom was at work and my sister was not home. He told me I had been really bad and I needed to learn a lesson. Something did not seem right so I tried to run. He grabbed me and hit me in my tummy. He pulled my shorts off. Threw me over his knees and at this time I was crying. He said, "It is ok. I love you. This what love is. Now stop crying or I am going to give you something to really cry for." I did not stop. This made him more angry. He said, "I will give you something to cry over," and he spanked me hard first with his hand then with a belt. I screamed as he covered my mouth. And he asked, "Tell me you like it, tell me you love me." I knew it was wrong, but at least someone was showing so kind of affection. After he whipped me harder, he screamed, "Tell me."

I said, "I love you."

He said, "And?"

I said, "And?"

"I said what!" I cried out in pain. He said, "Do you like this?" I said yes. He said, "That's my girl." He stood me up and said, "You going to do what I say now." I lowered my head and nodded; there was no way to escape. He hugged me. He turned around and blindfolded me.

I said, "Wait, please."

He said, "Be still, it is funner this way."

I again asked why.

He tapped the bed. He laid me down on the bed and turned me over and tied my arms together tightly up, then he pulled me back on my back, put my legs apart and stuck his finger up my thing. I asked if this was going to hurt. He answered, "At first yes." I was so tight. Tears came down my face as he moved in the bed. It did not just hurt a little. He said, "Let's see if we can loosen you up some." He tapped me and said, "With practice you will loosen up." It hurt so bad. I begged him to stop. He kept telling me how bad I was and this would make me a good girl. He said, "After a while that the cherry is not ready to pop, but we will get there." He said, "You see, good girls bleed." I said I was sorry. I tried. He said, "That's ok, we will get the other way. I was made to turn over and he whispered in my ear, "Do you want to bleed?" I begged him no and started to scream. He put a strip around my mouth with a ball that fit in between my teeth. He pulled me up on all four legs and stuck a hard object in and out my butt. I hurt. I could not believe the pain. I was bleeding and bad blood was pouring down my butt. He kept pulling it in and out as he whipped me. I kept trying to fall on the bed. He held me up on all fours. Hitting me as hard as he could. He said, "Stay on your knees. Beg for mercy!" Screaming, "You like that?"

I shook my head no.

He said, "Get used to it." He got a bit out of my butt. He screamed, "Well next time if you mind I will use a little oil," then he laughed and said, "Maybe not." He said, "I like this." He laughed and said I bleed like a pig. And then when he was done he untied me.

I took off the mouthpiece and he looked at me and said, "You make me sick. Get cleaned up, you pig." As he was leaving he said, "I will see you in a few days for our next date. You tell anyone and well you'll *pay dearly*."

I fell to my knees and prayed, "What do I do?" I got up. I went into the bathroom and I cleaned up really well. Then went to number 2 and all that came out was blood. I cried.

All this went on until i was twelve. IT HAPPENED AT LEAST FOUR TIMES A WEEK. And yes, he finally popped my cherry. He took something from me I could never get back. I could not even give that to my husband. And yes, I told my mom at the start. ALL THE REPORTS TO CPS DISAPPEARED. Because my grandfather was on the board of the police department. This only made me mad. The only way I could deal with things was drugs. So at the age of twelve I started smoking pot with my mom and her boyfriends. I used drugs from twelve to thirty-nine. Maybe I was wrong for using drugs, but it was that or end my life.

I called my dad at twelve years and told him I wanted to live with him. After a hearing in front of the judge, I finally got to live with my dad for a while. But he did not understand my mental health. Like my cutting. He gave me three chances then I was going to the hospital and each time I would be in trouble. The first time I had to write 1000 times I would not cut it. That was nothing. The second I got the belt bad with the hook too. I screamed, "Daddy, please!"

He said, "Don't 'Daddy, please' me. You did this to

yourself. Go to the center of your room!"

I said, "Daddy!"

He grabbed my arm, pulled me over to the middle, and said, "Listen! Can you hear me? I want you to grab your ankles. Every time you rise up the count starts over. Do you understand?"

I said, "How many, Daddy?"

He said, "Fifty. Now take your pants down."

"I said, "Please!"

He said, "Do as I say or the number goes up!"

I released my bottoms and took them down to my ankles, begging one more time.

He looked at me and said, "Make that sixty."

I was in trouble. There was no way out of this. All I could do was take it. I bent over and grabbed my ankles. My father whipped that belt around with loop and all. I screamed.

He said, "Count!" I said "One" then he hit me again. I screamed "Two". This went on until we got to about thirty. The pain was too much. He came around with thirty-one. I released my ankles, and before he could stop, I covered my bottom with my hands. The belt and hook hit my hands.

I screamed. "Daddy, please, no more!"

My father was mad! He said, "Up! Get up!" I stood up. He said, "What is wrong with you?" He took me, bent me over his knees, dropped the belt, pulled down my underwear and laid into like a madman. He said, "This how you wanted it instead?" Instead I kicked and screamed. The more I fought, the harder he hit. I stopped moving. He said "Hey" and pulled my face up to his. I had passed out from the pain. He pulled me on the bed and said, "Baby, I am sorry." Tears were falling from his eyes when I came to and he was sitting on the end of my bed.

I said, "Daddy?"

He grabbed me in his arms, saying, "I am so sorry, baby. Please forgive me. It will never happen again, I promise you that."

That was the last beating I got from my dad. He tried to understand me more. It was not like my mom; this man had a soul.

The third was the worst. My father sat me down and said he was going to do something bad. I did not understand. He said, "This is going to hurt me more than you." My stepmom pulled me to the kitchen and my dad poured a whole can of salt over my wound. I cried out in pain. This was killing him. How could I be so mean? And only think of myself. My stepmom was just crying too. The two people who took me home did this too. The ones that saved me from my abuse. And here I am abusing myself. And try to wash it off. He made me sit there for fifteen minutes with the salt eating at the cut. It was so painful. Tears clouded my dad's eyes and we fell to the floor together. He said, "If you cut the wrong way in the wrong area you can die."

I said I did not care.

He said, "I love you so much, boo boo. Can you understand this please?"

I said I was sorry and would try to do better.

"Just listen to me. You're my boo boo, why?" he asked as I saw the pain in his eyes that hurt more than the salt. It was like a knife going through my heart. I Wanted so badly to die at that minute.

I said, "I am broken. Damaged beyond repair."

He said, "All things can be repaired."

I said, "Not me." My dad held me forever and said we could fix this. I said I did not think so. He said, "Can we try?" I said yes. We had a long talk my way into my appointment. I said I would try. I had to see my counselor and she told my dad his actions were wrong.

He said, "What do I do?" We came up with rubber bands. We left the office. My dad took me over to the office supply store and bought me the biggest of rubber bands they had. Then told me to put them on every day. I must have had sixty rubber bands on each arm. Then we got a Happy Meal and went home. My father still did body checks on me to make sure I was not cutting. He would make me take my clothes off and make sure there were no cuts. Until we both felt safe. I did not mind. I had nothing to hide, this way we were both on the same page.

I lived in the house with my stepbrother Ricky. I do not talk about him much; he had a disorder that put him in a wheelchair and a bad heart. I always stuck up for him. He was my hero. He died at thirteen years old. I remember going to his school. There were a few kids that picked on him. I got in a fight because they pulled him out of his chair and were kicking him. I got upset and told them to stop. One of the kids ran off and the other asked me,

"Bodyguard, what are you going to do about it?" I grabbed the guy by the back of his head and smacked his head in the locker and broke his nose. We both expelled. My father was mad. He said fighting was not the answer. I got in trouble. I got badly beaten. I did not care.. My butt sure did. It will heal. I am always on for sticking up for others. Even if you do not win. Or you cannot sit for a while. My brother loved me sticking up for him. That was what was important.

Everyone was happy but we still had another problem. I wanted to wear my clothes to bed. My dad wanted me in P.J.s. I could not do that. He begged me. I said no. He took me upstairs to my room and took all my clothes and left me with my P.J.s and one sheet. He said wear them or nothing. I did not sleep at all that night. I was afraid too. I just cried and cried and cried. I was having a panic attack. I moved my drawer against my door and sat in front of it with no clothes on. My dad was mad I blocked the door. He came in screaming, "If there is a fire you cannot get out."

I said, "I don't have any clothes. What's the difference?"

He said, "Stop acting like a three-year-old."

I said, "You took all my clothes."

He said, "I really don't understand you at all. Do you want to go back to live with your mom?"

I said, "No, Daddy, please."

He said, "My rules in my house. No objects in front of the door. Are we clear?" I said yes. He said, "Now here are some clothes. Get dressed and get downstairs."

I said, "Yes, sir."

He said, "Call me Dad. Smart one."

Again I told my dad I was in trouble, and then I said the f word. My dad said, "What did you say?"

I said, "Nothing."

He said, "I heard what you said. Come here now." I was in trouble. He repeated, "What did you say."

I said, "F——."

My father looked at me and said, "Not in my house. He said go and pushed me towards the bathroom.

I said, "Dad, this is not a big deal."

"Not a big deal?" my father said. I was making him more upset. I figured I better shut up. All I was doing was digging myself in deeper. He said, "This is a Christian home. We don't use words like that around here." He grabbed a bar of soap and said to eat it.

I said, "I am not putting soap in my mouth."

He pushed the soap in my mouth and said, "Hold it there until I tell you to take it out." He watched his clock. After five minutes he told me to take it out, to rinse and go to my room. He said I was not having dinner. He would be upstairs to talk to me in a minute. I already knew what was going to happen. I was getting another beaten. This time I was wrong. My dad sat down on my bed. He said, "You know I love you, but I just can't help you."

I said, "What?"

"I don't understand mental health," he said. "I am sorry. I called your mom. I think it is best if you go back there."

I said, "Dad, please, I can change."

He said, "My mind is made up. You leave tomorrow. Pack tonight please." Once again I messed up. So they gave me back to my mom. It's not my dad's fault he didn't understand mental health.

There I was back with mom and on drugs. I was just misunderstood. But the weed was not doing it any longer so I got hooked on pain pills.

At the age of sixteen I had my first left knee surgery. Then I found pain pills. It was a downfall from there. I had six left knee surgeries. Then I went pill hopping.

At seventeen I got married. Big mistake. But I figured I traded one abuse for all those that would be nothing. Boy was I wrong. He was bad news. He ran trains on me with people to make money.

My dad was in and out of my life my whole life. I loved him a lot, but he didn't understand mental issues very well. I guess I destroyed him too. I must have been in 60-70 different mental hospitals growing up. I think I used that as a way too. I liked to have people put their hands on me so when I was in the hospital I would act out to get tied down, and of cause then came the shoot and the board.

Every relationship I get in is because of my past. Mom always taught me if a man didn't hit you he didn't love you. Who can blame me? I am damaged goods. So I left my husband and moved to another state. I tried to bring my best friend with me, who was in an abusive relationship too, but she would not leave him. After moving to Ohio, I found out she died in the relationship. That killed me. I tried to save her.

I got to Ohio still using drugs, got clean a few times but relapsed. That was my way out. Deals were my coping skill. I got some work for a while. I got in more bad relationships that caused me damage. It got to the point where I could not sleep in my bed or shower. I have not showered in my tub for five years or slept in my bed for four years. Do you know what it is like not being able to shower? I lean over the tub to wash my hair. Because I can't look at myself and the things that have been done to me. I can't sleep in my bed because of the nightmares.

I had one great relationship here in Ohio. He was a great man, but he had a fentanyl heroin addiction. It killed him. Well I killed him. He was so sick he needed a push and I gave it to him. I watched as he started to stop breathing and we got him to the hospital but it was too late. I killed the man I loved more than anyone in this world, my soul mate. Why did God let this happen? Now I am alone. I will never have anyone like him again in my life. I wish so badly I could take that back. No one can understand what this feels like. The pain I feel every day of my life. I took someone's life. And it was not mine to take. I can still feel his hair. The things we did together. The crazy way he would make me smile when everything was going wrong. We had a song towards the end; it was called "Saving Amy" by Brantley. He loved to cuddle too. I miss that I don't have that now. I have to stop talking about him now. I can't deal with this. I just miss him so bad. I lay here night after night dreaming of what we had. We will never have that back. I do not know if I will ever find anyone again. Sorry…

I used more heavily for a long time to deal with this.

December 17th, 2022 will be two years he is gone. That's two years too long.

On June 22nd, 2022 from abuse and trying to kill myself, I was in the hospital. That is when I met my first guardian angel, Tyler Furrie. I cannot say enough about this man. What could have been the end of my life was a chapter. He sat down and asked me why I wanted to die then found out the story. I just lost it and tried to kill myself in the ER two times. He said if I didn't stop he would have to tie me down. I got admitted to the hospital and called him from there and promised I would never do that again. After I got out of the hospital Tyler and his girlfriend Jackie built a relationship that led me to Christ. Tyler kept me in the TLC away from my mom so I could get clean. I started drug class and got sober. Jackie saved me from abuse. My ex did really bad things, and Jackie pulled me though. Jackie was there when I took pills for pain. She also came to my house to spend time with me more than once with her cat. She picked me up from doctor appointments when she had to work.

Tyler did something unheard of to keep me sober. Tyler became my medical power of attorney on my back because I could not trust my family. I only had Tyler, Jackie and God while I was in the hospital for over a month. They both came to see me in the hospital. I was supposed to have one surgery. That turned into four. I was very sick and my two angels stuck by me, as did God.

I died during one of the back surgeries. I came back in the ICU and had no family, only me and God. I have a war wound on my back. An imprint from God. I am back home recovering with Tyler and Jackie. If it was not for these two people I would be dead. No doubt about it. I can never repay them for what they have done. All I can say is God gave me the most special people I could ever have. I will never forget these people as long as I live.

I have IV antibiotics for a little while longer, but I am okay. God will take care of me. I plan to get my GED and go into some kind of work. I have many things I want for my life, but what does God want? I am so much stronger in my faith and walking with the Lord is crazy. I just praise God for everything and it's an attitude of gratitude. Never take anything for granted. Be blessed in all the things you do. Find happiness. Do good works. I feel like life moves so fast and people really miss out on life's good things because they focus so much on the bad. The world is full of bad, it really is, but it does not want it in the world.

All that matters is you. How are you going to react to things? What are you going to do? Try to think about others and how they feel. You are not the only one who has ever had a bad life or had a hard time. Pick yourself up, dust yourself and try again, only this time harder. I am not saying life is easy, it was never meant to be, but don't give up. Don't count the cost. Give it your 120% and don't look back, Just keep going. When you get down, keep going. When you are going to have to fight harder, kick more steam loud, whatever it takes, but don't quit.

Quitters never win. Winners are what we want to be. Work hard, stand strong and believe in you because you are what is important. God didn't make quitters. He wants you to work hard and believe in yourself just like he does. He will carry you when you fall, but he wants you to walk if you can.

Let me tell you something: I was in a wheelchair before my surgery. I was going to have one back surgery. It turned into four. I came out in a wheelchair then went to a walker. Now I am learning how to walk again on my own. Now that's God. I didn't give up. I wanted to make sure I would try someday but I didn't. I am slowly walking.

If I can go through what I have been through in life and still be here today to move forward, anyone can. I have been in some of the deepest, darkest times in my life and am still here to walk hand in hand with God. Anyone can because if he is for me who can really be against me? The devil is not stealing my joy. I will make it. I will come out on the other side. I worked too hard to give up now. Life sucks. Suck it up. Move on. And be a better person because of it.

Am I a writer? Maybe. Am I poem writer? Maybe. I'm a preacher. Who knows what i can do. I know there's no stopping me now. I love to write; it is a good outlet for me. Is that my calling? I don't know. I know I love to help people. That's important to me. I love people. I am a kind person. I would do anything for anyone. I am nothing like my mother at all. I see a lot of my dad in Tyler. Maybe that's the first thing that brought us close. I am not sure, but I thank God every day for the very few people in my life right now. They have given me so much hope and poured into me, that is just another reason I cannot give up. All these people who have put so much time and effort into me. I don't want to disappoint them. They are my life now besides the number one God. How could I give up now? It would not be fair. These people are so important to me. I would love to make this book in memory of all those people that have helped me. That have been there when no one was. Tyler, Jackie, my case worker from Ravenwood, my sister, my church, all these people who have my best wishes in mind who have led me down the right path. Home healthcare, Adam, all these people. They have all played apart in my life. They are all special people. And truly deserve to be blessed. I cannot thank them enough.

I spend my days thanking God for the blessings in my life and the changes that he has made in me. You know people ask me if i could change my life and do it over again would I. My answer is no because even though I have had a hard life and it sucked it made me who I am today. A kind, caring, loving person. I may not have ever gotten a high diploma, but I know more about life than most people would ever learn. And that is what makes me me. I am okay with just being me. I don't need a gold star or a medal or to be famous, I just need to help others find their way. Lead them to the Lord and tell them even if you have been abused you can still be okay. There is still light at the end of the road and you can be whatever it is you put your mind to. Never let anyone stop you from your dreams. Your dreams are as small as you make them and as big as your mind can carry them. You have the power to make all things possible. With work and trying your best, no one can stop you. I am amazed at how far we have come in this world. It is truly a blessing and curse. Some people are so mean while others are so kind. The devil is behind every corner. We go out and see all kinds of bad deeds and very few good ones. I have a hopeful heart that more people will come to the Lord before it is too late. I want people to know we have a forgiving God. And you don't have to be afraid. The Lord will forgive you and you will be set free. It took me a long time to learn that. I always thought God could never forgive me. And held so much hate too. But in order to move forward, I had to give that to God. That was harder than the abuse, just letting go of the hate. Because you don't want to feel hurt and hate but how can you just forgive? I mean read what happened to me and then to just say "I forgive you." It took a long time to get to that point and still there are some things I have not forgotten. I forgive but have not forgotten.

Anyways, some great news. Remember in my story I told you I had not been in my bed for years? Today, October 22nd, 2022, my angels Tyler and Jackie brought over my new Christian bed set. It has a loin for protection and it has the name Jesus with a saying on it that says, "My God is my king, my Lord, my savior, my healer, my refuge, my provider, my strength, my defender, my protector, my peace, my joy, my everything." So this morning at 8 a.m. I got to sleep in my bed! And I slept until 1 p.m. Now that's God. I am no longer afraid of my bed. The Lord is here to protect me. It feels really nice to be in bed again. I feel like I have so much power back over my life. I don't think the shower is gonna be so easy. I am going to get there. God willing.

I have a mental disability and a learning disability and a physical disability but that has not stopped me yet. See, I am on social security. But I choose to work. I will not just get a check handed to me. I am not lazy. My mom thinks I should just collect a check. I am not like that. I want to earn my money. I like to work. It gives me process and meaning. I write some great poems. My next book is going to be on my poems. I want a closer walk with God. I ask for that every day. There has never been a moment that I feel I am walking alone. I always feel loved by God. No matter what I am walking through, he is always there. God is so beautiful to me. I truly believe God does not make mistakes; he loves you just the way you are. Nothing you ever do could ever change how he feels about you. If people only knew how great our God is. If I could hear God say when I was young how much he loved me. If people could only hear God say how much he gave for us to be free. If people were not so blinded by worldly things. And they just listened a little more. Sometimes we don't just need to pray but we need to listen to God. He answers prayer but not if your mouth is still moving. So give him time to answer. God does not care if you are mad; he wants you to pray anyways. He wants to hear from you.

When I lost the man I loved in my life, I cried out to God. God hears our every need. I told him how I felt. I let it all out. I said, "God, you're really going to take him?" I felt God took my heart and ripped it to pieces. I lost my mind about how God could have done that. Yes, we were bad for each other, but we were happy. Now I am alone again. Am I ever going to find someone? It's God just laying with me. Does he want me to be alone my whole life? I just want happiness. Something I will never find in myself. It's not fair. I am not asking for a miracle, just someone to spend my life with. I hope God has something great in store for me. Other people can be happy. Why can't I? No one wants me. I am disposable. God is the only one who has not thrown me away in the trash yet.

Notice that I said *yet*. I love God. I don't think he would do that to me. I go to church every Sunday. I wish we had church more often. In all things that have happened to me, I feel like I need to spend all the time with God as possible. I wake up every day thanking God for one day to live and breathe and worship him. I pray often probably more than most do. I read my Bible though this app I found; it could be a Bible gateway. It reads my Bible though audio and I follow a long, because to be honest, I don't know how to read or spell. I am on a fifth grade reading level, but that's okay. God never told me I had to be smart to be accepted by him. Thank you, Lord, for that.

I can't count how many weeks it took to learn this IV. I broke bags. I am still getting the hang of it. I struggle daily thinking I will never be good enough, smart enough. But I put those limits on myself. I know with hard work I can do anything. Yes, I struggle a lot and it's not fair, but who said life was fair? No one. The greatest thing for me to remember is I can do all things through Christ who strengthens me. He will never leave me or forsake me. He will walk with me. Hold my hand when I start to fall. And carry me when I am weak. That's our God, our one true, amazing, loving God. He will never leave you in your time of need. Everyone else may leave you. You may lose your job, you may lose your home or your family if you got one, you may lose cars, money, anything, everything, but you will not lose God if you follow him.

When everything seems to be falling apart, turn to God. He knows what to do. He will guide you all the way. Let him be your light. I am going to tell you something. It may sound silly, but I bought 70 cheap WWJD bracelets and I put four on at a time. Two on each arm. When I look down is a constant reminder to ask myself, "What would Jesus do?" I ask God everything: What to wear. How to act. What to eat. I go to him over the silliest things, but I know he does not mind; he loves me. And I'm glad to hear from you. When I am in pain, I cry out to him to relieve my pain. He hears me. I know he feels my pain and tries to help. I cry so much. Trying so hard not to take those pills, trying to be stronger. It hurts so bad sometimes I want to give up. But I just can't. My feelings are so real and I am emotionally damaged inside by my past and my pain. I just keep leaning on God hoping that one day I will find peace of mind and freedom from pain. I am not asking for too much, just for a little bit of caring and love from God to know he is there.

It has been so hard to write this book about my life. It has brought up a lot of things from my past. It has opened wounds that never healed. I want to know why no one ever helped me when I was younger. They could have. Now I am left with broken damage beyond repair. I hurt a lot. I know we go through things in life to make us stronger, but I was wrong, really, really wrong. Still to this day my mom tries to take it from me. I had to get a lawyer and get my money protected so she couldn't take it. I am coming in with some money but my mom wants it. She made me pay off her old car. And now she wants me to pay off her new one. She used her boyfriends and husbands our whole life, but for her to use her kids, I can't believe her. For real. Stand up and be an adult for once in your life. Quit using other people. Why are you doing this? Do you have no values? My mom makes me so mad. She is a user. I have had enough from her and she wonders why we do not have a good relationship. She is toxic to my mental health and my sober living. I have tried with her so many times and gotten nowhere. I tried buying her love and everything. It just does not work. How can you make someone love you when you do not even know what love is or how to love yourself?

This book is good for me because it shows me so many things about myself. I do not trust people I can't. I need to but I can't. It's just not in me. To trust means I have to let someone in and how can I do that? Everyone I ever trust has hurt me in the past except Tyler and Jackie. And of course God. I pray one day I can be free of all this bondage of my past and learn to love, but to be honest, I have let Tyler and Jackie in, but I am just waiting for the day they turn on me too. I should not say that. They are great people. It's nothing against them, it's all me. I am so scared I will never find anyone in my life and be alone my whole life, but that is my fault because I will not let anyone in. God, please, I beg of you, fix this wounded heart of mine. Let me trust again. I fear what my future holds like this. I do not want to die alone. I could have all the money in the world but that cannot buy love. Is my future lonely? I hope I do want someone so bad. Do I not belong with someone? I will just continue to wait on God to find me someone. I hope he answers fast. Until then I will just continue to pour into him.

Put God as number one. God will change your life if you let him. Being alone is not bad; some people need time to grow. Some people need to grow for God, others for themselves. I just think I need to work on myself and God right now. So I think I also need to focus on being more positive. I have a problem with negative thinking. I always think the worst. I have to stop thinking everything is going wrong. Just give it to God and let it go. There is nothing I can do about it so give it to God. And let it go. I believe God is going to take care of me. I do not have to worry about anything. See, in order for me to move on with my life, I had to heal. I had to tell myself it was okay to love again that I could forgive. Not forget but forgive. Because if I want God to forgive me I have to forgive others. I told God, "You want me to forgive these people, you have to help me because I do not have it in my heart." So it took a long time but I forgave. And a sign of freedom came over me. I was free of all that hate. And let me tell you something, hate will eat you alive. The pain, the guilt. But you get a sign of love that fills your heart. I am so free now. I just love the Lord more every day. He counts on me to do things in my life to show me he loves me, cares and will always be there. I will forever be grateful to my Lord for changing my life and saving me from my past, washing away my sins and keeping me safe in his arms all these years. I am so undeserving of his love and grace and mercy. My greatest fear is that I will fall short of his love and do wrong. I pray that he will pick me up and put me back on track and his punishment will not be too much for me to take. I know he is a loving, forgiving God and I know I will sin. I am only human, but I hope he will forgive me. I have problems and fall short sometimes. So my prayer is that God teaches me to do the right thing all the time. I want to be smart and strong in the Lord.

Never sin, always know what is right.

My nights are the worst times for me. That's when I really start to feel down and hopeless. I am so lonely. I try to keep my head up but sometimes it's hard. I feel like I am beat down a lot. I try to stay in the Lord's light. Think tomorrow is going to be a better day. I feel defeated. And I try hard. I just need to sing out to the Lord. Maybe pray and ask the Lrd to cover me with his peace and love. God, why am I not happy? Why am I so sad? Is it my mental issues? I am grateful; I am just sad. My chains are gone; there is nothing bonding me any longer. Maybe I just need to get on my knees and surrender to you. Ask you to fill me up again, Lord, like a mighty storm awakens my soul again. Do not let the devil steal my joy. I want to know you more, my Lord. I am so weak and tired I lay at your feet in tears. Just please, Lord, fix what is broken. Make me whole again, well more like make me whole for once. Have your way in me; please change me, please, Lord. HOW DO I FIND MY WAY! I just need to lean on you, my Lord, there is no other way. Please, Lord, carry me. Help me! All my God, the pain. The loss. The rejection. It's not fair that I have been done this way. This is only part of my life, there is way more to it. I tried to work and I was fired because of my mental issues. At one job. Then I tried to work at another job and got fired because I could not read. Then I got another job and got legal problems for serving alcohol to a toxic person for real. The guy came, got his own beer, showed me his ID paid, and did not smell. I lost my job because he was 2% over the legal limit. How about you put a breath tester in these stores? So I try to make a living and this is what happens. No one ever gives me a chance. I had to go to court over that and of course the charges were dismissed but it is still on my record. And when I went in front of the judge he ordered me to pay court costs. I asked if I could speak. He said yes. I said, "I will pay court costs but I lost my job so the court cost is coming out of my social security which is all your taxpayers' money." I said thank you.

I just fall on the Lord a lot because I get depressed. I do have good times but not always. I am still healing from my back. That's a problem. I just do not want to give myself bad hope. I just need to stay more positive for sure. I know the Lord loves me and can bring me through this. I just need to ask. I am needed and the Lord will be there. He has helped me before and he will now. I am going to ask him for a complete healing. I know he can do this. He can and he will. I believe he is going to do great things for me. I will not give up. I am not a quitter; I never was. I am a strong person. I have been through hell and back and am not stopping here. People have abused me, stole from me, fired me. Put me down, used me, not wanting me to break my heart, my trust, but I got the Lord. And that's the biggest tool in my tool box. He has saved my life over and over and over again. And you know what? He is still here. He feels my pain. He was there in everything I went through. Picked me up and carried me on his shoulders. He never left me lonely.

Thank you, Lord, for loving me, for caring. I made you this promise: Now I see you have never left me, I will never leave you and I forever put my trust in you. That is the biggest thing I can do: give you my love and trust. And, Lord, I hope you know how hard this is for me. I will forever walk with you. I give you my all. My life, my breath, my heart, my soul. I ask you to forgive me of all my sins, great and small. Wrap me in your arms and love me for just me. Please, no strings attached, I am all yours for good. I love you, Lord, and will always be grateful for all you have done. You will always be my number one!